# Caring for Your
# Fish

Lynn Hamilton

**Weigl Publishers Inc.**

**Project Coordinator**
Diana Marshall

**Design and Layout**
Warren Clark
Katherine Phillips

**Copy Editor**
Heather Kissock

**Photo Research**
Gayle Murdoff

Locate the water bubbles throughout the book to find useful tips on caring for your pet.

Published by Weigl Publishers Inc.
123 South Broad Street, Box 227
Mankato, MN 56002 USA
Web site: www.weigl.com

**Library of Congress Cataloging-in-Publication Data**

Hamilton, Lynn A., 1964-
  Caring for your fish / Lynn Hamilton.
      v. cm. -- (Caring for your pet)
Contents: Fishful thinking -- Types of fish -- First fish -- A fish's
life -- O-fish-al decisions -- Tanks for everything -- Food for fish --
Water bodies -- Cleaning -- Healthy fish -- Fish behavior -- Fish
stories -- Pet puzzlers.
  ISBN 1-59036-035-4 (lib. bdg. : alk. paper)
 1. Aquarium fishes--Juvenile literature. 2. Aquariums--Juvenile
literature. [1. Aquarium fishes. 2. Fishes. 3. Pets. 4. Aquariums.] I.
Title. II. Caring for your pet (Mankato, Minn.)
  SF457.25 .H35 2002
  639.34--dc21

                                    2002006160

Printed in the United States
3 4 5 6 7 8 9 0  06 05 04

**Photograph Credits**
Every reasonable effort has been made to trace ownership and to obtain
permission to reprint copyright material. The publishers would be pleased to
have any errors or omissions brought to their attention so that they may be
corrected in subsequent printings.

**Cover:** aquarium fish (Aaron Norman); ©**Anthony Bannister/Gallo Images/CORBIS/
MAGMA:** page 11 top; ©**Brandon D. Cole/CORBIS/MAGMA:** page 10 top; **Comstock
Images:** pages 17, 23; **Corel Corporation:** pages 9 top, 9 bottom, 27; **Daorcey
Le Bray:** pages 13, 22; ©**Lawrence Manning/CORBIS/MAGMA:** page 12; **Aaron
Norman:** pages 3, 4, 6 left, 6 middle, 6 right, 7 left, 7 middle, 7 right, 10 bottom,
11 bottom, 14, 15, 16, 18/19, 21, 24, 25, 30; **Picturesof.net:** title page, pages 28, 31;
©**Michael Pole/CORBIS/MAGMA:** page 5; **Reneé Stockdale:** page 20; **Royal Tyrell
Museum/Alberta Community Development:** page 8; ©**Walt Disney Pictures/
Photofest:** page 26.

# Contents

Water World  4

Pet Profiles  6

First Fish  8

Life Cycle  10

Picking Your Pet  12

Tanks for Everything  14

Fish Food  16

Water Bodies  18

Fresh Fish  20

Healthy and Happy  22

Fun for Fish  24

Fish Tales and Fins  26

Pet Puzzlers  28

Frequently
Asked Questions  30

More Information  31

Words to
Know and Index  32

# Water World

People enter an enchanting underwater world when they look through the glass of an **aquarium**. It may seem like a quiet place, but an aquarium is an active **ecosystem**. An aquarium is a complex water world. All living things in an aquarium, including fish, plants, and **bacteria**, affect each other. Even the non-living items in an aquarium, such as gravel and rocks, play a part in the ecosystem.

Fish are highly sensitive to water temperature and condition. These should be monitored to keep your fish safe and healthy.

■ Aquariums are often home to several different kinds of fish.

Fish come in a variety of types, colors, shapes, and sizes. They also have a variety of needs. Caring for fish involves more than sprinkling food in a tank. Fish cannot meow or bark to let you know that there is something wrong. You must learn to recognize fish behavior patterns and signs of distress. It is a good idea to have your pet registered with a **veterinarian** in case she becomes sick. By carefully selecting fish, plants, and accessories, you can create a soothing and comfortable home for your water pet.

■ Your fish will rely on you to meet their food, water, and health needs.

## Fascinating Facts

- Tropical fish originated in two warm-weather regions called the tropics. These two regions are located on either side of the **equator**. Hundreds of varieties of tropical fish are now kept in home aquariums. People choose them for their bright colors and beautiful patterns.
- More than 20 million people in the United States have home aquariums.

# Pet Profiles

**T**here are thousands of types of fish from which to choose a pet. New types of fish are still being discovered. Some types of fish live in cold water, while others can only survive in warm water. Many fish do not get along with other fish.

## GOLDFISH

- Many different varieties
- Often orange, golden, or red, but can come in many colors and shapes
- May live from 5 to 25 years in a home aquarium
- Cold-water fish; they thrive in water at 65° Fahrenheit
- Hardy fish that can adjust to a range of conditions; some can live in outdoor ponds
- Normally peaceful; will chase smaller fish

## GUPPIES

- Males come in a variety of colors and patterns; females are usually gray
- Have attractive, colorful tails and fins
- Are 1 to 2 inches long
- Swim in the middle area of the tank
- Can adapt to a range of conditions, including some variation in water temperature
- Peaceful with other types of fish; often picked on by other fish

## ANGELFISH

- Common angelfish is silver, with black striped fins and sides
- Flat and oval in shape, with long, pointed fins
- Up to 5 inches in length; grow quickly
- Graceful swimmers
- Good fish for beginners, but are often raised by **aquarists** with more experience
- Community fish

Knowing what type of fish you want will help you to plan the aquarium. Many fish owners choose freshwater fish. Freshwater fish require water that does not contain salt. The chart below shows a few of the fish suitable to the beginner aquarist.

## MOLLIES

- Come in a variety of colors; the black mollie is a favorite
- Some types may grow to be 6 inches long
- Require some salt in their water; about 1 teaspoon of salt per gallon of water is best
- Like to nibble on plants
- Feed from the surface of the water
- Disease prone
- Usually peaceful; may chase smaller fish

## TETRAS

- Come in a range of beautiful colors; neon and cardinal tetras are popular
- Usually between 2 and 3 inches long
- Can live up to 4 years
- Get along with friendly fish of a similar size
- Do not like brightly-lit tanks; prefer shady tanks
- Normally peaceful; some types may chase slower, smaller fish

## PLATYFISH

- Often red; other types include black, tuxedo, and sunset platyfish
- About 1.5 to 2.5 inches long
- Often bump against the glass with their lips when hungry
- Like to nibble on **algae**
- Not very demanding
- Hardy
- May require some salt
- Peaceful, but not timid; do not bother any other fish

# First Fish

Fish, the earliest **vertebrates**, first lived about 500 million years ago. By that time, fish had developed armor plates and scales for protection from **predators**.

The Age of Fish began about 410 million years ago. This age saw an explosion of fish diversity. Larger fish with strong jaws developed. The first bony fish appeared. Over millions of years, new types of fish, such as sharks and rays, emerged. Most of today's fish are descended from fish that lived almost 250 million years ago.

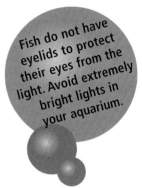

Fish do not have eyelids to protect their eyes from the light. Avoid extremely bright lights in your aquarium.

■ The coelacanth first appeared more than 350 million years ago. It has not changed very much.

### Fascinating Facts

- One type of fish, called coelacanth, was believed to have died out 70 million years ago. In 1938, it was discovered that fishers in South Africa had been catching the fish for years.

Many years ago, humans used nets and spears to catch fish for food. Before 2000 BC, humans were raising oysters and fish for food. Soon, people began to keep fish as pets for their beauty. In Egypt and Rome, fish were kept in ponds. Over time, more and more fish were kept as pets. Goldfish were popular in China in AD 1200. Spreading to Japan, then Europe, keeping goldfish as pets became popular in North America during the 1800s. The guppy first appeared in Europe in the early 1900s. Around the same time, angelfish arrived in North America. Today, clubs, associations, and magazines offer information to fish lovers everywhere.

■ Throughout history, humans have caught fish for food.

■ Sharks and rays are members of the fish family. There are nearly 375 types of sharks.

# Life Cycle

All fish begin life as eggs. Guppies are livebearers. This means that they hatch their eggs within their bodies and release the live **fry**. Goldfish are egg-layers. Egg-layers release eggs that float in the water. The eggs are attached to something in the water or hidden among plants.

## Eggs

For livebearers, **incubation** lasts between 1 and 3 months. The mother should not be disturbed until she is about to give birth. A bulge under the gills means that a livebearing mother will give birth in a few days. She should be moved gently to another tank. Eggs from egg-layers are tiny. They look like bubbles or jelly. Some fish parents leave their eggs unattended, while others guard them. Other adult fish will eat the eggs, so the eggs need to be protected.

## Maturity

A fish will continue to grow throughout his life. Generally, the larger the fish, the longer his life span. Goldfish can live up to 20 years if properly fed and kept in clean water.

## Fascinating Facts

- Hundreds to thousands of eggs are laid by one mother. This ensures the survival of at least some of the fry.
- Egg-layers may hold their eggs and fry in their mouth to keep them safe.
- Eggs are often colorless, making them difficult for hungry fish to find.

## Birth or Hatching

Newborn fry are only about 0.25 inches long. To keep out of danger, some fry will hide in plants, while others will drift to the bottom of the tank. The number of fry born to one mother can vary from 8 to 250. Some eggs from egg-layers will hatch within a day. Others may take weeks or months to hatch. Fry should be kept away from all adult fish, including their parents, until they are big enough to fend for themselves.

## Fry

With frequent, small meals and warm water temperatures, the young of livebearers can double in size during their first month. The fry of egg-layers are very small, so be careful not to scoop them up when cleaning the tank.

# Picking Your Pet

Usually when choosing a pet, people select one animal. When picking fish as a pet, you may find yourself planning a whole community. Your answers to the following questions may affect your fish decisions.

## Is My Home Suitable for Fish?

Even small homes and apartments have enough space for an aquarium. It is important to find a place in your home where your fish can be safe and comfortable, but also watched and enjoyed. Fish tanks should be kept far from frequent noise or movement. Family pets, such as cats, should be considered when buying fish. Be sure the tank is placed safely out of reach.

Overcrowding is dangerous, as bigger fish may eat smaller fish. A veterinarian can recommend a safe number of fish for your aquarium.

■ The larger the aquarium, the more it will cost. For first-time fish owners, a simple fish bowl is often the best choice.

# What Kinds of Fish Would I Want in My Aquarium?

To be safe and comfortable, fish in a tank must all get along. They should thrive in the same water conditions and temperatures. While you can mix and match the fish in an aquarium, this must be done with care. It is important to know which types of fish are friendly with others, what area of the tank they prefer to swim and eat in, and what plant life or rocks are needed.

## What Can I Afford?

Fish may not be costly, but aquariums are. You will need to buy a tank, equipment, accessories, food, and some cleaning supplies. You will need enough spare time to maintain your aquarium and care for your fish.

Decorations provide hiding spots for your fish. They help your fish feel safe.

## Fascinating Facts

- For beginner aquarists, a freshwater aquarium is easier and less costly to manage than a marine or saltwater aquarium.

# Tanks for Everything

As your fish's home, the aquarium must be safe and comfortable. This will keep your fish healthy and happy.

Small bowls are fine for some types of fish but are not suitable for others. Flat, rectangular tanks offer plenty of room to swim. A tank that is 24 inches long, 12 inches wide, and 12 inches deep is a good starter size. Tank covers prevent escapes and help keep the temperature stable.

A heater hung on the edge of the tank will maintain proper temperatures. Place a thermometer in the tank, far away from the heater. This will allow you to monitor the water temperature.

Ask for help when handling electrical equipment. Before working on or cleaning your aquarium, always unplug everything.

■ The size of your tank will determine the number of fish you can safely keep.

A filter helps keep the water clean and clear. Filters usually contain **carbon**, which removes waste and odors. The carbon has to be replaced occasionally. A small pump is also needed to force bubbles and oxygen into the water.

A well-rinsed layer of gravel about 2 or 3 inches thick may be placed along the bottom of the tank. Gravel holds plants and accessories in place. Rocks, wood, and ornaments, such as small ships or caves, can add interest to the tank and offer safe places for your fish to hide. Be cautious when placing things in your aquarium as some materials may be toxic to your fish.

■■■ To help your fish feel at home, choose plants and accessories that mimic your fish's natural environment.

## Fascinating Facts

- Light is important for the health of fish and plants. Between 12 and 13 hours of moderate light will match the night-and-day cycle of their natural environment.
- Plants provide hiding spots for fish and release oxygen into the water. Some fish like to nibble on plants. It is important to find out which plants are suitable for your particular fish before placing the plants in the tank.

# Fish Food

The feeding habits and needs of fish vary with each type of fish. Some types of fish eat plants, while others eat meat. Some fish eat both. Top-feeders are a type of fish that prefers to feed from the water's surface. Midwater-feeders are fish that prefer to feed from the middle of the tank. Bottom-feeders feed from the bottom of the tank. This information will influence the types of foods you buy for your fish, as some foods float and some foods sink. A treat of frozen food, freeze-dried food, or live foods, such as tubifex worms and brine shrimp, may be enjoyed by many types of fish once a week.

Overfeeding affects water quality. Wasted food will spoil in the tank, which may cause your fish to become ill.

Many food products, such as flakes, pellets, and tablets, are available at pet-supply stores.

Fish should only be given the amount of food they can eat in 5 to 10 minutes. Some fish will overeat, which can make them sick. A variety of food creates a balanced diet. Another aquarist or your veterinarian can advise you on the healthiest combination of foods for your fish friend.

■ Fish should be fed once or twice every day.

# Water Bodies

Fish have a pointed head and a body that narrows into a tail fin. This shape helps them travel quickly and smoothly through the water. Separate muscles along a fish's body control fins and the direction of travel. Fish have special senses that feel change in the movement of water and detect the presence of objects or other fish. Many other fish features help make them suited to underwater life.

The caudal fin is located at the end of the fish's tail. Moving the caudal fin from side to side helps propel the fish through the water and steer.

**- CICHLID**

The beautiful colors of some fish are due to their skin cells. Fish have developed an ability to change color to blend into their environment. This prevents other animals from seeing them. Other special skin cells produce a slimy mucus that makes fish slippery. Scales provide a protective body surface.

Dorsal fins are found on a fish's back. Anal fins grow on their undersides. Dorsal and anal fins help fish keep their balance and stay upright.

Water enters a fish's mouth and passes over the gills. The gills take in oxygen from the water and release the gas called carbon dioxide. Then, the water exits through the gill openings. Gills allow fish to live and breathe underwater.

Part of a fish's breathing process involves the lips. By puckering their lips, fish can pull water into their mouth. Lips are also shaped to suit the feeding style of the fish. The upturned mouth of a top-feeder allows the fish to scoop food from the surface of the water.

Pectoral and pelvic fins come in pairs. Pectoral fins are found on the sides of fish, behind their head. The pelvic fins are located behind the pectoral fins. The pelvic fins help fish stop and steer.

# Fresh Fish

Fish become accustomed to their water. Major water changes may cause stress, which can leave fish open to illness or disease. Replacing too much of the dirty water with clean water can be unsafe for your fish. Replace only one-quarter to one-third of the water, and clean the tank every week. Depending on your aquarium's needs, you may need to clean the water more or less often. You can buy kits that check and control water quality.

When moving your fish, avoid touching her with the net because a fish's skin is very sensitive.

■ To clean your fish's tank, gently remove your fish using a smooth-edged net. Place him in a temporary tank until his tank has been cleaned.

Algae may begin to grow in your tank. It can provide food for some fish. It may also make the glass of your tank appear dirty. Special scrapers are available to keep the glass clean. Bacteria also thrive in aquariums. Some bacteria are healthy. Waste is turned into less harmful materials by bacteria. Overcleaning the filter can remove too much bacteria.

Special vacuums are available that clean bits of waste from the gravel. Be sure to remove dead leaves from plants as they can also affect water quality.

▬ Snails, and some fish such as tangs and surgeon fish, help keep aquariums clean by eating algae.

## Fascinating Facts

- Fish release a gas called ammonia in their waste. If enough ammonia is present in the water, it may kill your fish.
- Detergents can be poisonous to fish. It is best to clean and prepare new tanks and accessories with salty water. It is also important to rinse the tank and ornaments thoroughly.

# Healthy and Happy

Only buy healthy fish. Avoid fish with sores, white spots on their scales, or bulging eyes. Fins should not appear damaged. Fish should be active but not frantic.

Slowly introduce your fish to the tank by letting him float in his bag in the tank's water for about 15 minutes. The water temperature in the bag will gradually adjust to the temperature of the aquarium. Your fish can then be transferred into the aquarium without unnecessary stress. Avoid adding several new fish to a tank all at once. One or two fish every couple of weeks is usually safe.

Filters remove medication from the tank's water. If treating a sick fish, filters may need to be temporarily removed.

Fish are usually carried home from pet stores in a plastic bag.

Sometimes, fish need to be moved to a **quarantine tank** when they are new, producing young, or ill. This prevents diseases from spreading. The move can be a frightening experience for a fish. Since a fish can be hard to catch, there is a risk of injuring your pet. It is easiest and safest to use two nets. Use one net to gently direct the fish into the other net. This should be done with great care.

Keeping your fish healthy includes checking for changes that may signal illness. Changes in color, fin, or gill condition, or a decreased appetite may be warnings. If you see any of these conditions, immediately ask your veterinarian for advice.

■ If your veterinarian prescribes medicine for your fish, be sure to follow directions closely.

## Fascinating Facts

- There are many ways to calculate safe numbers of fish for your tank size. One recommendation is 1 gallon of water for every 1 inch of fish.
- Fish have a special way of breathing underwater. However, a gasping fish is likely a sick fish.
- Tap water may contain chlorine, which is unsafe for fish. Tap water is usually safe for your fish after it has sat for a few days. Conditioners that remove chlorine from water can also be used.

# Fun for Fish

**D**ifferent types of fish will behave differently. Some fish, such as angelfish or swordtails, like to travel in **schools**. Some fish are aggressive toward other fish. One fish, called the Rosy barb, will nip at fish with long fins. Two or more male Siamese fighting fish will bite each other to death. Guppies usually get along well with other guppies and other types of fish.

Loud, sudden, or constant tapping on the glass can disturb your fish. Anxious fish are likely to become ill from these noises.

■ Male Siamese fighting fish will live up to their name when placed together in one tank.

## Pet Peeves

**Fish do not like:**
- non-stop tapping on the tank's glass
- being fed the same fish flakes every day
- ornaments that move suddenly
- never having any privacy
- cat paws dipping into the tank
- obnoxious, glowing, neon plants and ornaments

Many fish like to explore. Other fish prefer to hide during the day and emerge only at night. After disruptions, such as a tank cleaning or the introduction of a new fish, some fish may become stressed. For these fish, rocks, ornaments, and vegetation provide an essential hideaway. Other fish, such as goldfish, are naturally active and enjoy plenty of space in which to swim. They prefer that the aquarium not be cluttered with too many plants or ornaments.

■ Fish that hide during the day enjoy rock formations or hollow logs that are big enough to enter.

**Fascinating Facts**

• Most fish should be fed once in the morning and once in the evening. Feeding your fish at the same time each day, and from the same spot in the aquarium, sets a routine. Fish are creatures of habit. Soon, your fish will expect food at the regular mealtimes. She may even be waiting for you in the spot where she normally catches her food. This will become a fun activity for you and your pet fish to share.

# Fish Tales and Fins

Fish have appeared in myths and legends for centuries. One story tells of the first goldfish, who came from an ancient magical well in China. A Native-American tale describes a young girl who was turned into a fish by the Great Spirit. Although she briefly becomes human again, she soon returns to the water life she has come to love. Legends have told of beautiful creatures called mermaids. They are part human and part fish.

■ Disney's cartoon mermaid, Ariel, was torn between the land and water worlds she loved.

## Fascinating Facts

- Public displays of marine and freshwater fish are found throughout the United States. These public aquariums also research fish. Tours and programs help educate the public and work to protect **endangered** fish.

Humans have tried to recreate some of the fish's special features so that they can travel underwater. Many people scuba-dive to observe tropical fish in their natural environments. Some divers use fins to propel themselves through the water world. They also wear wet suits that can withstand cold water temperatures that fish are naturally built to endure.

■ Scuba divers need a mask, fins, and special equipment to breathe and position themselves underwater.

## Why the Fish Has Scales

This folk tale from the Philippines tells of a farmer and his wife who had a baby girl. They loved their daughter so much that they showered her with affection and refused to let her do any work. She grew to be a beautiful maiden. Often, she would admire her own beauty in the reflection of clear streams. One day, when the king of crabs asked to be her friend, she refused, telling him he was too ugly. He jumped out of the water and scratched her face. To soothe her sores, she splashed water on her face. This caused the scratches to turn into scales. The king of crabs had put a spell on the maiden, turning her into a fish. Today, it is said that fish will quickly jerk away from their own reflections, because they remind the fish of their lost beauty.

# Pet Puzzlers

What do you know about fish? If you can answer the following questions correctly, you may be ready to own a pet fish.

**Q** Why should fry be separated from adult fish?

Fry are very small, weak, and helpless. Adult fish, including the fry's own parents, will eat eggs and fry.

**Q** How much food should I feed my pet fish?

At mealtimes, fish should only be fed as much as they can eat in about 5 to 10 minutes.

**Q** Can tropical fish share a tank with other fish?

Tropical fish come from warm-water regions around the equator. As a result, they require warm water in their tanks. So, they can only share a tank with other fish that thrive in warm water.

**Q** What are weekend feeding blocks?

Weekend, or slow-release, feeding blocks allow fish owners to leave their fish unattended for a period of time. The blocks are designed to gradually release food into the water.

**Q** How should accessories and plants be chosen?

The plants, gravel, and accessories with which you choose to decorate your tank should reflect your particular fish's natural environment. Some fish require places in which to hide, while others need wide, open aquariums for swimming.

**Q** When should a fish be quarantined?

New fish, sick fish, or fish having young should be separated from the other fish in the tank.

**Q** When cleaning the tank, how much water should be replaced?

Fish become used to their water. No more than one-quarter to one-third of the dirty water should be replaced at one time.

## Future with Fish

Before you buy your pet fish, write down some fish names that you like. Some names may work better for a female fish. Others may suit a male fish. Many names can be used for either male or female fish. Here are just a few suggestions:

Aqua    Bubbles

Siren

Goldie    Flounder

The Fin    Jaws    Sebastian    Matilda    Scales

# Frequently Asked Questions

### Does my fish sleep?

Fish do sleep. Their eyes do not close, but they are likely able to ignore images. It is normal for some fish to rest sideways on the bottom of the tank. Others will remain afloat with their fins moving to hold them upright.

### Can I leave my fish unattended?

If you are careful to clean the tank and check all equipment, such as pumps and filters, most fish can be left alone for a weekend. Slow-release feeding blocks help. For longer absences, a friend should care for your fish while you are away. Be sure to leave detailed instructions. That way, your friend will not overfeed your fish and will know what to do if your fish becomes ill or the equipment breaks.

### Where is the best place for my aquarium?

While it is nice to look at a tank at eye level, reaching it for cleaning may be difficult. The tank should be placed on a steady surface, near an electrical outlet. It should be placed out of direct sunlight and away from heat sources and drafty areas. Make sure the tank is out of the reach of young children and pets. Water weighs about 8 pounds per gallon, so choose a surface that can support the tank's weight. Moving your aquarium can be inconvenient and may disrupt your fish. Choose its permanent location carefully.

# More Information

## Animal Organizations

You can help fish stay healthy and happy by learning more about them. Many organizations are dedicated to teaching people how to care for and protect their pet pals. For more fish information, write to the following organizations:

American Aquarist Society, Inc.
Box 100
3901 Hatch Blvd.
Sheffield, AL  35660

Humane Society of the United States
2100 L Street N.W.
Washington, DC  20037

## Web Sites

To answer more fish questions, go online and surf to the following Web sites:

### Care for Animals
www.avma.org/careforanimals/
animatedjourneys/animatedfl.asp

### Pet Planet
www.petplanet.com/

### VetCentric
www.vetcentric.com/

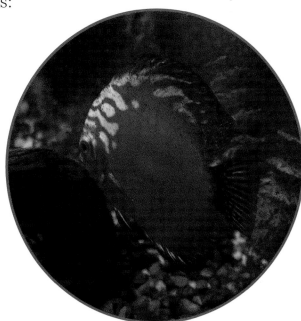

# Words to Know

**algae:** green, slimy growths that develop naturally in an aquarium, often collecting on the glass

**aquarists:** people who keep an aquarium

**aquarium:** a container, such as a tank or bowl, in which water animals and plants are kept

**bacteria:** one-celled organisms that can only be seen through a microscope

**carbon:** element found in all living things

**ecosystem:** a community of plants and animals

**endangered:** animals whose numbers are so low that they are at risk of disappearing from the world

**equator:** imaginary circle around Earth midway between the North and South Pole

**fry:** newly hatched baby fish

**incubation:** the time before hatching when young develop within the egg

**predators:** animals that hunt and eat other animals for food

**quarantine tank:** a container that temporarily houses fish to separate them from other fish

**schools:** groups of fish that swim together

**vertebrates:** animals with backbones

**veterinarian:** animal doctor

# Index

**algae** 7, 21

**aquarium** 4, 5, 6 ,7, 8, 12, 13, 14, 15, 20, 21, 22, 25, 26, 29, 30

**cleaning** 11, 13, 14, 20, 21, 25, 29, 30

**filter** 15, 21, 22, 30

**food** 5, 9, 13, 16, 17, 19, 21, 25, 28

**freshwater fish** 6, 7, 26

**fry** 10, 11, 28

**goldfish** 6, 9, 10, 25, 26

**guppies** 6, 9, 10, 24

**health** 4, 5, 14, 15, 17, 21, 22, 23

**life cycle** 10, 11

**pet peeves** 24

**saltwater fish** 7

**supplies** 13, 14, 30

**tropical fish** 5, 7, 27, 28

**veterinarian** 5, 12, 17, 23

**water temperature** 4, 6, 11, 13, 14, 22, 27